AMERICA'S
Patriotic
Poems and Prose

A Tribute to our Flag, our Service Men and Women, and our Fallen Heroes

G&L

PUBLISHING

These poems and prose of inspiration and national pride
were written to honor our gallant troops
involved with the Persian Gulf War,
and all our wars that were
fought, so that our great country
would always remain free.

———————————

Twenty-five percent of the profits
of sales of this book
will be donated to funds and scholarships
assisting families of soldiers who gave their
lives in the Persian Gulf War.

"God Bless America"

George Shea

CONTENTS

CONTENTS

FORWARD

by George Shea

This book is dedicated to the President of the United States, George Walker Bush. His courage and decision to launch the liberation of Kuwait inspired me to write my first poem.

The variety of this collection is obvious; it spans from poems dedicated to noted individuals to prose on truth; every person I dedicated a poem to or titled one for was especially moving to me during the Persian Gulf Crisis.

To those who served their country, committed to freedom. To all who gave their lives for this freedom especially, Specialist Cindy M. Beaudoin, Connecticut National Guard and Lance Corporal Daniel Byron Walker, two casualties who remain in our minds as do all heroes in everyone's home town and state.

I would like to thank all the people directly and indirectly who gave of their knowledge, suggestions, time, energy and criticisms.

I owe a special debt to Millie Gault, Directorate of Operations and Planning at the Pentagon for her practical advise and encouragement.

To Major Stephen Foster and Captain Michael Barron, Department of Military Instruction, West Point Military Academy, for the many informative talks we have had concerning military procedures and logistics.

To Sgt. Roland Hall and P.F.C. John Harasti, Fort Hood, Texas for their friendship and humor, yes I will drive a tank and fire a cannon.

A special thanks to Mr. Jim Vinchetti and Mr. Ed Peruta of Community Television Channel 32, of Rocky Hill, CT, for airing my poems and prose, and to their continued excellence in reporting and encouraging community patriotism.

To all the military wives, husbands, sweethearts, families, support groups and military bases throughout the country, thank you for your support and creative inspiration. This is the foundation for which our country continues to thrive and stand against injustices in the world. With people like you, this great country of ours shall always be number one.

Amo Te Vera.

George Shea
Wethersfield, Connecticut
July 4, 1991

INTRODUCTION

by Arlene Shea

One man's expression of patriotism, materialized in the form of a collection of poetry and prose. As it happened that man was my brother, an avid historical researcher and writer but George had never written a poem before the Persian Gulf Crisis. His trust in his president and his freedom of choice as an American allowed for the possibility that his thoughts could be published.

Struggle and strain in acceptance of a possibility of war effects each one of us differently. Uncertainty makes us examine our beliefs, George's examination drove him to talk to government officials, to pursue an active letter writing campaign earmarked for the troops in the Gulf, and even more involving design his own strategic defense and attack plans. His war poems were composed between December 1990 and June 1991, an intensely creative time.

He is the quintessence of "Being an American", one who holds his government, leader, and fellow man in the highest regard, one who gets involved. I am very proud of my brother and applaud his integrity and personal expression of patriotism. He's truly a Connecticut Yankee Doodle Dandy.

Arlene Shea
Wethersfield, Connecticut
July 21, 1991

POEMS

HAIL PRESIDENT BUSH

A mad man far across the sea
Tried to dominate you and me.
He's barbaric as they come.
Hussein is his name.
His claim to fame
Would be his shame.
In our land is a Navy hero
Who took a stand.
He said no one will ever
Invade our land or those
Across the sea who believe in democracy.
That we would fight
To protect our rights and those
Of others who didn't have the might.
Some media and others said he was wrong
But as you can see
They were barking up a tree.
He pulled the country together.
The parades and rallies honoring
Our troopers are a sight to see.
I'm proud as a peacock
To have a leader such as he.
He prays and cares for those we love
Who may get the call from above.
Navy hero that you are
You came very far.
You soar higher than a star.
You are a man who did his all
To defend our proud land
So it would always stand.
The thirteen then and fifty now
Still fly high because men like you
Way back when held that staff
Never to let it fall
From their grasp.

WHO WAS HE

He joined the Army
So he could eat
Three squares a day.
Things were tough on the street.
Good jobs were hard to be had.
He worked hard at what he did.
Fighting on foreign soil
To keep our land free from tyranny,
He rose through the ranks
And became the first black
To become the chairman of the Joint Chiefs of Staff.
This great man contrived the plans
With our leaders in the Pentagon.
Not Armageddon as some said it would be,
We came out with victory.
Because of him the war came
To a quick end.
Many lives were saved because of what he did.
This modest hero deserves our praise.
Our country thanks you General Powell
For your knowledge, grace and military prowess.
This will always keep us free
From those who wish to keep us down
And let our flag fall to the ground.
Now we know who he is,
A shining star in our midst.
Thank you again General
And those in the Pentagon
For a feat that shall
Never be beat.

THANK YOU GENERAL STORMIN'NORMAN

There's a General across the sea
He's a lot bigger than you and me.
He looks taller than a tree.
As Joyce Kilmer said years ago,
Only God can make a tree.
If that be the case
Then we'll see that it had to be,
As the tree was made by He.
We can say this great leader
Was sent to you and me
By the maker of the tree
To keep us free
And never be on bended knee.
He fought before on foreign shores.
But after that who was He,
A soldier defending you and me.
But then we knew when we
Saw him on T.V.,
What he was and what he could do.
He loved his troopers
And worried about their cares.
He was their big teddy bear.
Onward he had to go and plan the attack
Which we were to behold.
This brave, courageous, calculating man
Put it all together.
He was on the front lines where
Seconds, not minutes
Determine whether men live or die.
His decisions saved many from
Hearing that final bugle call.
This General of ours did it right
And put the enemy to flight.
Many great battles have been fought through the years.
History will say this one has no peers.
You see General, God made that tree.
We thank him, that's the way it had to be.

RIDE ON DAN QUAYLE

He's a talented, handsome young man.
Being second in command of our land.
He goes about his job
Bothering no one, doing the best he can.
He's not in the limelight at all
Because his boss gets the calls.
He's the second stringer
And sits on the bench.
If something happens to the starter,
He will go in and the responsibility will be his to bear.
He traveled the countryside to military bases
and other places, speaking to all,
Giving them hope so they wouldn't despair
And worry about their loved ones over there.
When the war was finished
The media came into the picture
Concerning the presidential race.
They don't seem to care what they say
Or who they offend.
The military were asked by them
If they wished to run for Vice President.
Not caring for the feelings
Of our second in command,
He shouldn't be put down
His job was well done.
This is lowbrow and tasteless,
No tact at all, as to what they did.
For their information, President Bush
Could run alone and not even campaign and
Still win the election for what he did.
Thank God the Pentagon ran the war
And not those we see on T.V.

MARINE CHIEF WARRANT OFFICER
CHARLIE ROWE

The President and the rest of the country
Saw your noble deed on T.V.
You were trained to kill
And defend our land.
What you did will long stand.
You showed compassion for your fellow man.
Our enemy you met.
Upon surrendering, instilled with fear
and afraid of death,
They humbly begged for their lives
As you held your forty-five by your side.
I believe one kissed your hand,
Another one tried.
You said it's alright, it's alright,
With caring and love in your eyes.
The time wasn't right to kill
And take life away.
There was something Godly in you
That made me look and say
I'm very proud to have
This special Marine represent me.
When they were on bended knee
The one above had to say
He is worthy of me.
He made my day, what more can I say,
When he uttered those beautiful words
It's alright, it's alright.
God Bless This Noble Marine.

THE GALLANT MARINE

Dedicated to:
Marine Lance Corporal, Daniel Byron Walker,
Who Gave His Life for His Country
In The Persian Gulf War

When his mother watched him grow
As a child she held him close.
His hurts and cares were hers to bear.
As mothers often do
They give and never take,
For deep down there is something
They seem to grasp.
It's a strong Godly force
Full of love that will always last.
This young man joined the corps,
Young at heart, in prime of life.
He had to do what he thought right.
He went across the sea
To fight for you and me.
His country called and he gave his all
He paid the supreme price
In battle he fell with no more life.
Because of him our flag
Will always stand tall and never fall.
The Gallant Marine from Texas
The Lone Star State is that star.
As he too and other fallen heroes
Are the stars in the Red, White, and Blue.
In my heart he will never die.
As his mother holds the flag
Where he is laid to rest
She cries for him
As I did too.
But from above Dear Mother of Him
Do not despair.
Your son will be honored by He,
The maker of you and me.

OUR HEROIC LITTLE GIRLS

Dedicated to:
Specialist Cindy M. Beaudoin
Connecticut Army National Guard
Who Gave Her Life For Her Country
In The Persian Gulf War

Our little girls, we love them all.
When they were small
We watched them grow tall.
They'd run around, frolic, and play,
with their pigtails hanging down
Almost touching the ground.
They were happy as can be
Nary a care to trouble them.
When they grew tall
And knew about life
They had a certain call.
They joined the Army, Navy, Marines, or
Whatever their choice may be.
Our President said our country
Calls you now.
Across the sea they went
To protect you and me from tyranny.
They knew their lives were on the line.
For those brave who fell
The Lord would say,
Many are called but few are chosen.
You the chosen are now with me
Where you deserve to be.
When I see a small girl playing around
Her pigtails almost hitting the ground,
It will be you I see,
Because that's the way it's meant to be.
In my eyes you will never die.

DEPARTMENT OF DEFENSE

Carol Drury, Deputy Director Of Community Relations
Major Shelley Rogers, Tour Director, Public Affairs

The courteous Marine
Whose behind the scenes
Along with Carol
Are hardly seen.
The reason being they are on the phone,
Answering calls from those
Who need advice on matters of protocol
And affairs that have them up in the air.
The Department of Defense
Is where they're at.
Public affairs are their cares.
They relate to you and me
When we don't seem to
Grasp certain facts involving our military.
They do their best
To put our mind at rest.
It seems like the one above
Gave them that special knack
To put us on the right track.
When all is said and done,
They will hang up the phone,
It will ring again and
A voice will say, Public Affairs
What are your cares.
Thanks to those we never see,
Their satisfaction comes
From pleasing you and me.

THEY SOARED ABOVE ALL

They fly high into the sky.
A bird could never do this with its best try.
They fly so fast it's hard to see
Where they will finally be.
They maneuver about with such ease
you'd think they're playing hide and seek
With the clouds as they go in and out.
But don't be fooled when the time is right,
They will be there to answer our plight.
The time did come we need say no more.
The enemy ended up on the floor.
The pilots of these planes of ours
Displayed courage that will carry them far.
We saw on T.V. what they did.
It shall never be hid.
They were called to fight and did it right
and put that mad man Hussein's army to flight,
Causing disorder among them all
So they would fall.
They bombed the enemy night and day
Making it safer for our ground forces
To live another day.
Many will say I'm here today
Because those in the air
Answered our prayer.
These are the heroic pilots
Who are where they should be,
High in the sky close to He
Who made it possible for them
To soar above all
So they would always stand tall.

THE COALITION STOOD FIRM

Who were these brave men and women?
Where did they come from?
Why were they there?
They came from all walks of life,
British, French, Italians and others
From nations that believed in liberty.
The United Nations said something must be done
To stop this madman Hussein from taking
Control of a free land.
He was told to leave
But wouldn't heed to the might we had.
President Bush, cool as could be,
Let it be known there was no backing down.
A Vietnam this would never be.
He gave the order, all lands of the free
Jelled as one.
They hit hard and fast.
No way would Hussein ever last.
His Army was beaten.
Kuwait was free at last.
The coalition stood firm
In spite of decries from T.V.
That many would die.
If Armageddon was to be here
Like some have said,
How wrong they were.
The good Lord had his say.
You'll have to wait another day.
Free nations in due time will adhere
And pave the way to make this world
A safe place to stay.

THE UNITED STATES FIRST CAVALRY

Dedicated to:
Captain John Roper and
Those Who Serve With Him

Where does it begin.
Does the origin have no end.
We can't say this.
Because many years ago, they were there.
They fought and fought and stood tall.
They would fight to the last.
To insure that no one
Would ever be on bended knee
And die needlessly.
Yes, they are now across the sea.
The cavalry that was here years ago
Is over there protecting you and me.
The horses may not be there
But what occurred long ago, soars above all.
General Custer gave himself up.
400 of General Terry's own would live
Because of what he did.
They ride today, maybe in a different way.
The cavalry is here to stay.
They are second to none.
As the brave get the call
They do honor to us all.
Because of them, we shall never fall.
God Bless the United States First Cavalry.

COMEDY OF ERRORS

How wrong can they be.
When we watched T.V.
You saw and I saw
What was going on
Far across the sea.
All these so-called experts
And Monday morning quarterbacks
Made it a comedy.
Our great leader President Bush
Was called a wimp.
Marines were going to land by sea.
Worst of all, 50,000 or more of ours
Were to die if we choose to attack on land.
The Republican Guard was praised so high
You'd think they were Rommel's best.
They fought 14 year olds and those
Ready to go on Medicare.
It was said by some that Armageddon was to come.
The military press conferences
Were something to bear.
Thank God our leaders
Had the patience of a saint.
A ten year-old child wouldn't ask
Some of the asinine questions
Put to them by those in the audience.
Praise the Lord, the Pentagon ran the show.
If those on T.V. held the reins,
Hussein would be here by now
Causing us much pain.

Media, pseudo experts and Monday morning quarterbacks
remember this. If there should be another war, I
couldn't take two comedies in a row. The reason we
lost in Vietnam was because the war was run by the Media
and politicians, not the military. Render unto Caesar that
which belongs to Caesar. Render unto the military that which
belongs to the military. In plain English, butt out. Have a
nice day!

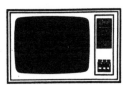

WHY ?

As the sun sets over the Persian Gulf,
We wonder why they died.
Our land it wasn't,
On foreign soil were we.
The land was barren,
A tree you never see.
It was hot as can be.
The brave we lost.
They fought and died for a noble cause.
Mad man Hussein was stopped in Kuwait,
If not he would have dominated other lands.
Another Hitler would he be.
If that be the case, his missiles would be
Coming at you and me in our land of the free.
Our fallen heroes knew that.
They knew some wouldn't come back,
Saying this is why we died.
We had no choice, there was no other way.
Those we love will live another day.
Our fallen heroes are somewhere above
With the one we love.
He called them there and are in his care.
Loved ones cry for those they lost.
It's hard to bear, but those in His care
Say don't despair, we're with the one
Who made the sun.

THE UNITED STATES NAVY

Their ships roam the seven seas
Every day constantly protecting you and me
From our enemies.
Their jobs are many to say the least,
Transporting our troops and supplies
To lands where the fighting be.
When a landing is to be made
From the sea they shell enemy positions
Night and day paving the way
For those that land to have a
Better chance to walk away
And live another day.
The aircraft carriers are a sight to see,
Big as can be they carry the planes
That bring destruction upon the enemy.
The sailors are the ones we seldom see
Being far away from the naked eye.
They're in the turrets or down below
And many places that we don't know.
Yes, they are there in that mass of steel
That floats upon the sea.
The ships go because of them.
The skills and knowledge that
They have learned makes them
The best of the rest
When upon the brine they sail.
May his hand hold them above
And never under let them go.
Without them this Country
Would have a tough road to hoe.
Bless them all.

THE PROTESTERS ARE WRONG

They wave their banners and march up and down.
They never seem to have their feet on the ground.
They yell and scream and want to be seen.
Only fools would do what they do.
The President and Congress say we must
Fight to protect our rights.
Better to wage war on foreign soil.
Let it be there or you will see
What it's like to run for your life.
When bombs upon you fall
Your loved ones will die before your eyes,
Then you will say I wish I chose
The other way.
Hussein kills his own with gas.
Not satisfied with that
Missiles are sent out.
The innocents of Arabia and Israel
Feel his wrath.
The Persian Gulf he floods with oil.
Only a maniac would do something like that.
If we don't stop him now,
In due time he will have that awesome bomb.
So you who protest, let me see
If that be the case
How can you stop it from coming
Across the sea at you and me.
Think twice before you yell and scream,
The next time you do could be your last
From that terrific blast.
Cowards die many times before their deaths
The valiant never taste of death but once.

PATIENCE OF A SAINT

Honorable Dick Cheney, Secretary of Defense
Honorable James A. Baker, Secretary of State
Honorable Pete Williams, Undersecretary of Defense Spokesman
Lieutenant General Kelly, Army - Brigadier General Neal, Marines
Those from Great Britain, Saudi Arabia and others I can't recall.

We thank you for a job well done.
As we watched you on T.V.
You kept us well informed
As to what was going on.
I don't know how you kept your cool
When asked questions by so many fools.
If they had their way
Hussein would be here today.
They should know that strategy, planning
And military moves are known only to us.
In God we trust and no one else.
You had the patience of a saint.
You never gave in as you were asked
When we would attack and other
Asinine statements that would set us back.
You were men who showed a lot of class
In what you had to do.
It was my pleasure and I'm sure the country's too
Watching you as you kept us abreast,
Under the conditions of war,
Giving us information that you were able to.
Patience is a virtue.
Thank God it applies to you.

HONORABLE DICK CHENEY
SECRETARY OF DEFENSE

We saw and heard so much of him.
He was here, there, and everywhere.
To the Persian Gulf he went
To make sure when the attack was to come,
Our enemy would be on the run.
He did his task true to form,
What more could we ask.
His responsibility is very big indeed.
Those he oversees are the Army,
Navy, Marines, Coast Guard, Air Force
And who knows what's in between.
He's cool, calculating and smart as can be,
Just what our great country needs.
We thank the one from above
For giving us such a man
Who gained our love and admiration
For what he did for our great nation.
When put to the test
He did his best.
Those under his control
Went on a roll,
Victory was ours.
He made it look easy,
Because it was planned right.
If done wrong it is hard, and many would die.
A place called Nam will attest to that.
If he were there, in six months or less
We would have won.
You see, if it's done right,
They would have been put to flight.

SANDS OF IWO JIMA
TO THE SANDS OF KUWAIT

The call is made again
By our President
For these gallant men to protect our land.
At the given time they will shine.
There's a tyrant across the sea.
Hussein is his name,
And he's crazy as can be.
He's threatening all those
Who believe in democracy.
He cares for no one, not even his own.
He wants to bring us down.
But this will never happen,
Because we have a great fighting machine
Called the United States Marines.
As they have done before
When we were first born,
They put the enemy to flight
When our nation was engaged
By those who tried to take away our rights.
They fought with all their might, and
To this day their honor, glory, and
Bravery can never be denied.
They are one of a kind,
Very hard to find.
As the good Lord gave them to us,
They are proud as can be,
As they should be,
For they are the United States Marines.

TROOPERS IN THE SUN

The troopers are there far across the sea.
They left their land to protect you and me
So We'd always be free.
They shall stop those who oppose the rights of all.
Causing them to fall where they stand,
Never to reach our land.
Their despotic control will never hold.
The day will come when the sun looks down.
They won't be seen,
For buried deep they will be.
An early grave, as you see.
It had to be, they will never torment the free.
The troopers have much to endure
The days being hot and long.
The sand too blows through the air
Causing much despair.
But they shall hold their own
For all will come to pass
Tyrants never last.
Hitler and others bit the dust,
Hussein will go in a land full of sand.
We are proud of our troopers across the sea.
Our prayers are with them constantly.
May the good Lord hold out his hand
And bring them back safely to our land.

> Like the song says
> God Bless Them All

OUR FLAG

Our beautiful flag flies above
Fluttering in the breeze.
Chills go up and down my spine
When I realize what it means to me.
She's saying care for me
And you shall always be free.
I'll never let you down,
As long as you don't let me
Fall to the ground.
Love me as I love you,
Then one we shall be
United forever as family.
I was torn, worn,
And bent, but never broke.
From 1777 when I was born
To the Persian Gulf in 1991,
The good Lord watched over me.
Because of this, I still fly high.
I look and smile with great pride
Upon you all.
Many thanks come from me.
You remained as one,
That is why I'm still here and
Endured through the years.

THE UNITED STATES ARMY AIRBORNE

Their basic training is rough and tough.
The art of killing is a must.
This they do or don't survive.
They are highly trained in what they do.
If that's not the case, a difficult task it would be
To protect you and me.
They're a special breed,
Not many are able to cope with their feats.
Into planes they go soaring in the sky.
Behind enemy lines they jump
Taking a chance where they land, in a stream or tree.
This is dangerous as can be.
They have no fear and do what they must.
When they hit the ground they engage the enemy,
Blow up bridges, infiltrate or
Whatever the plan may be.
Their job is always well done
Bringing honor and glory to our free land.
Our country thanks these gallant, brave,
Heroic ones who seem to jump out of the sun.
I especially thank the good Lord for them.
If that were me ready to jump out the door
Looking down at the ground,
I'd end up passing out lying on the floor.

THE BRAVE WHO SERVE

We shall always honor you.
You who represent the red, white, and blue,
We are proud of what you do.
Our hearts are full of joy
When the Stars and Stripes go flying by.
For what we see brings us to bended knee.
It is you who are the stars
Fighting to keep our country free,
So never in bondage we'd be.
There are a very few
Who don't like what you do.
They say that it is their right not to fight,
They burn the flag
But they shall learn,
If no flag there be
They would be the ones
Burning like a tree.
So you see, you brave who answered the call
You are right after all.
May the good Lord bring you safely home to us,
That will be the final plus.

THE PRESIDENTS FAMILY

Our boys and girls were over there.
Yes, I call them boys and girls
Because to a father and mother
That's what they would always be.
To them they never grew up.
They're still their little babies
As when they were first born
And held upon mommy's or daddy's knee.
Their love for them will never die
Because they are family.
The family was made by He
The maker of you and me.
A call was made by a man
To defend the rights of all.
He will go down in History for what he did
As the greatest of this century.
President Bush is his name
And his claim to fame would be
That he stood by his family
No matter what the situation may be.
His family was across the sea
Defending you and me.
They were Whites, Blacks, Spanish, and
You name it from all walks of life.
He called upon his family
You saw what they did.
The family held together,
The rest is History.
We lost a few brave that were there,
Even one causes us much despair.
Those little babies who became
Fully grown gave their all
To keep our country free.
The greatest tribute we can pay
To them is to look on high
And see the Stars and Stripes go flying by.
We say thank you and God Bless You,
For deep down our great family will never die.
Because you gave your all
We shall never fall.

I LOVE MY TROOPERS

I love my troopers for I am the Red, White, and Blue.
I sent you to a far away land
To protect our rights and those of every free man.
All nationalities and races
Comprised this gallant band.
From all walks of life you came.
You answered my call and gave your all,
The days were hot and the sun beat down upon you.
The nights were cold.
The sand would blow in your face,
Making you wish you were never in this place.
When the battle came
You moved forward at a fast pace,
Attack you did with such devastation
The enemy was routed.
Victory was yours in no time at all.
History will say the battle here
Will have no peers.
There were fallen heroes
As in every war.
My heart cries out for them
And their families too.
Remember one thing I'm here because of them.
They are the stars in my Red, White, and Blue.
Without them I fall,
No longer standing tall.
I say thank you and God Bless You
To all my troopers for what you had to do.

DID HE DISOBEY ORDERS ?

*My good friend Augie Pizza served with the 82nd and
101st Airborne with honor and dignity during World
War II. Here's the story he tells. You be the judge. Did
he or didn't he?*

During his tour of duty
Many jumps he made.
Into battle he went,
Young and fearless as can be.
The Germans were his enemy.
A place called Bastogne was where
He and others made a gallant stand.
On a hill he was, his company fighting
Against overwhelming odds.
The Germans were coming from
The left and right.
The airborne kept fighting
With all their might.
The enemy was drawing closer,
The Captain yelled out, fix bayonets.
Augie turned to him and said
This I cannot do.
The Captain with his eyes glaring said
I order you to fix your damn bayonet.
Augie replied, Sir, with all due respect,
I can't fix my damn bayonet because
It isn't broken.
I had to get this one in.
Thank you Augie.
God Bless You All.

OUR BEAUTIFUL RED, WHITE, AND BLUE

As the Red, White, and Blue hovers above
We look in awe at that which we love.
She started off small
And grew through the years.
She now has fifty stars.
They didn't come without scars.
There were those who tried to tear her down
And let her fall to the ground.
Not only from our enemies across the sea
But those from within who did everything
They could to express their idiotic whims.
But that didn't work, for she's still here
And will be long after they're in eternity.
When she feels she's going to be hurt
She cries out to us,
Knowing very well we'll do that which we must.
We won't let her get tattered and torn
And thrown to the ground.
Answering her call we'll give our all,
So she'll never fall.
When our task is completed
We'll look toward the sky.
Our Red, White, and Blue
Will be fluttering on high
As proud as can be.
Somewhere from above He seems to say
There can be no other way.

MAD MAN HUSSEIN MUST GO

The commandos must come in.
Needless to say, this is the only way.
From what nation they be
It matters not to you or me.
If not known they wish to be,
Their secret will be kept by the free.
He must be destroyed,
He was the destroyer of many.
He killed innocents
And God's creatures in the sea.
He thinks he's above all.
In due time he shall fall,
When the commandos get the call.
I hope and pray that day
Is not too far away.
An animal he can't be called,
They are better than he.
When he gets his, I'll smile and say
You dirty S.O.B.
It couldn't happen to a nicer guy.

BRAVE MEN All

Many brave men were called,
Many brave men were to fall,
They had to be there, but they didn't care,
Their land was in despair.
They gave their all so we'd never fall.
What they did shall live on.
Pain and suffering they had to bear,
Their bones were shattered and battered beyond compare.
They held their own and made it known
That no one would ever take our home.
We are here because of them,
They stood tall so we'd never fall.
So raise our flag as they did then,
Let it flutter above and wave in the breeze,
Then they'll say, we're here to stay,
Just look up, it's still there,
We didn't let it fall after all.

CAPTAIN CATHY LoPRESTI

She's warm and friendly as can be.
This I know for a fact,
As she talked to me.
Her phone is busy constantly.
She's in the United States Army.
Military matters are put to her
By those who call.
She answers one and all
At the U. S. Central Command
Where she's at.
It was my pleasure
Talking to her the other day.
She's very caring in what she does.
If she has the patience
To listen to me,
Some day a General she will be.

NOT YET - YOU PANICKED

It was years ago
October nineteen seventeen
When the beautiful Lady
Appeared to a little girl.
She was happy and filled with awe
To behold what she saw.
The Lady said she came from above.
Four statements were made
To the little one by her.
Three have already come true,
One remains to be fulfilled.
We don't know when the end will come,
Only He has the key.
But to erase any doubt and fear
That you may have,
The fourth has yet to come.
Without that there will be no Armageddon.
When the fourth does come,
Then time will tell
Where the place may be when
We'll end up in eternity.

FIFTH COLUMN ?

Through the years we've been in several wars.
Our brave were called to defend our free land.
They fought and died so that we would survive.
The enemy they fought
Were not only in the field.
Propaganda was used to sway their ways
By those across the sea
And those who live in our land of the free.
In a way you might say
The Fifth Column was back in play.
There were many who tried their ploys
To undermine our great land by what
They had to say.
To name a few we have Axis Sally, Tokyo Rose,
Hanoi Jane, and Bagdad Peter.
Our boys and girls died for our flag.
The above mentioned showed their class.
They belong with the trash.

FIRST SELECTMAN

Dedicated to:
Paul Sweet
Plainfield, Connecticut

Who is this man and what does he do?
He's not the President, Senator, Governor
Or whatever the case may be.
He's just a man of little renown
Who runs a small town.
He takes pride in what he does.
The town is small as can be.
Everyone comes together in time of need
It's one big family.
Those he loves go off to war.
Many he knew well.
A few years back
They sat on his lap.
When they come home, he plans the parades
And other events to honor them.
The hours are long and there is much to do.
It matters not for he loves them all
And prays to God that many didn't fall.
But some did fall and that tears him apart.
Deep in his heart he wants to cry
As they are laid to rest.
When he reads of their good deeds,
He honors them for what they did
To keep our country free.
Sir, when I write my poems
I feel the same as you,
I cry for those we lose.
The President when speaking on T.V.
Was on the verge of tears.
So you see, Paul, for what's involved
You and your town aren't
So small after all.
The wheels of the Lord grind slowly
Yet exceedingly small.

OUR HOMETOWN HERO

Air Force Sgt. Raul Wallace
Was one of the first
To come back to our land.
He grew up in Hartford, Connecticut.
Here he lived and played as a boy.
Into manhood he would grow.
He joined the service when of age.
When his country called
He did what he had to do.
He went overseas to protect you and me
And our liberties.
We thank the good Lord
That he is here today.
Because of this he was
Honored with a parade.
The hometown hero was
Proud as can be.
He has every reason
To feel that way.
But hometown hero
I have to take away
Some of the play.
I say this to you
As I'm writing now.
This is my hometown too, and
I'm just as proud if not prouder
As we all are for what you were
Called to do.
You kept our flag flying high
So victims of tyranny
We'd never be.

THE FIRST LADY

She's spry and agile as can be.
Her name's the same
As the man who holds the reins.
Barbara Bush be her name,
Married to George of Persian Gulf fame.
She's always there by his side
Giving him strength and spiritual aid,
So his long hard day will be easier to bear.
Knowing she is always there,
Gives him that extra drive
That comes from within.
When outlooks seem grim,
They turn into wins.
His cares are many, she knows that.
She does what she must without any fuss,
Making speeches, going on tours,
Visiting hospitals, traveling our land,
Bringing joy the best way she can.
She wears pearls all the time,
On her they look mighty fine.
Up above are the pearly gates,
Only He has the key.
So you see He opened the gate
And passed on to her the love
And warmth which she gives to all.
The pearls she wears
Are a sign of that.
This I believe for a fact.

PRESIDENT BUSH GET WELL

We love and honor you,
Especially those who went across the sea
To fight for democracy.
You brought the country together
In time of war when worry besought all.
You too worried much,
The pressure had to be unbearable.
Stress and strain to you came.
You did it your way.
Many lives were saved to live another day.
Your prayers and concerns
Were always for them.
Night and day you were on call
To make sure our brave over there
Would never in jeopardy be.
One life lost would be too many.
We saw the love and worry in your eyes.
When on T.V. you spoke,
From the heart it came.
Our great President you are,
But the compassionate man in you comes from Him.
He held his arms out as you did too,
Bringing those He loved to Him,
So they could stay another day.
Our love and prayers are with you Mr. President.
The one above will watch over you.
This He shall always do.
The love and compassion you showed
Your fellow man will always stand.
I say this with pride.
I'm honored to have you by my side.

THEY BELONG TO THE RED, WHITE, AND BLUE

We were in a war some years back.
It was sad, tragic, and unpopular as can be,
The reason being it was run
By the media and politicians.
That alone will cause much despair.
Our military had little to say.
The troopers fought and died.
You can't blame them
For the blunders of the other two.
Our country was torn apart.
When they came home
No heroes welcome did they get.
Now we realize what they did.
We should always honor them.
They never turned their backs
On the Red, White, and Blue.
When our troopers come home
From across the sea,
Many parades there will be.
It would fill me with great pride
If our heroes back then
Would march with them side by side.
Whatever the case may be
Honor is due all
When they answer our country's call.
Their blood is the same,
That will never change.
It was spilled to keep our great land
Free from tyranny.

MAKE HIS DAY

He's up there in the clouds above,
Then clears the air to end our despair,
He moves his hand as fast as can be,
To bring the sun to you and me.
He knows light must shine, to give us time,
To see the way we make our day.
What we do and how we do it,
Will be answered on the day,
When we will have nothing to say.
He will call the play, to see,
If it's okay to be with Him on judgement day.
So above all, always stand tall,
You may fall, but never crawl.
Bounce right back and give it a whack,
Take what he gives you,
And what is left give as he gave,
For it will revolve as you can see,
Because you did it right you will have a good night.

Amo te vera

THE FAMILY'S STRESS

During peacetime, families and loved ones
Live in our land without despair.
When war breaks out
Their loved ones go far across the sea
To protect you and me.
Those in the combat area
Know their lives are on the line.
They also know their loved ones are
Safe and sound in the land of the free
And no harm will come to them
From the enemy.
Those who are here are filled
With worry and fear.
They know not where
Their loved ones may be,
If they will fall or be wracked
With pain from wounds suffered
When fighting the enemy.
They watch T.V. hoping and
Praying when casualties are reported
In certain divisions, their sons and
Daughters won't be there.
They sit at home wondering and waiting.
The pressure for them is hard to bear.
It's much harder to cope with here,
Than it is for those over there.
We are here safe as can be.
When it comes to that
Those across the sea are worry free.
Families here always fear that
Their loved ones won't come back.
They hope and pray that the good Lord
Will hear what they say
And bring them home
To live another day.

BETH, MARINE'S WIFE

When I call you with your group
Your soothing voice makes me feel at ease.
I get somewhat tired from writing
And sending my poems overseas.
This I must do for you and
Your crew at Applebees.
You are one big family
Called The United States Marines.
You are there as one,
Working and frolicking together,
Hoping and praying your loved ones
Will come safely home.
When all is said and done
And that day comes,
I will say thank you Beth.
Though we have never met,
It was my pleasure talking to you.
God Bless You and your Marine
And all those beautiful people at Applebees.
You all held on and kept your cool.
Our country is very proud of you.
I felt very close to those with you
As I did with others I got to know
And never met throughout our land.
I never wrote until now,
But it came to me and
I thank Him.
Because of this, I got to know
Many fine people in our Free land.

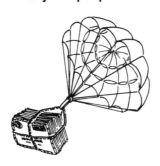

HAPPY MOTHER'S DAY

Your childrens' cares were yours to bear.
You loved them very much
As they were growing up.
You fed and clothed them,
A roof over their head
There always was.
When they were sick,
You were there to nurse them back
To health with loving care.
When they are fully grown,
Parents they will become.
The Godly love you gave will in theirs be.
Like a ray of light from above
It shines upon them.
There it will stay,
Being no other way.
It all came from a beautiful mother
Who shines like a star from afar.
She stands alone full of grace,
No one can ever take her place.
Our noble mothers, we thank and honor you
On this day especially and all days.
Some of you aren't here, we shed a tear.
We know that which comes from Him stays within,
In our hearts you shall always be,
For the love you gave shall always stay
And never go away.

THE WAR IS OVER

There are those who always keep moaning and groaning,
Saying how easy it was the way we won.
When done right, it's always easy.
When done wrong, it's always hard.
If this war were fought like Vietnam,
Our troopers would still be there
Fighting and dying and not knowing why.
If the war in Vietnam were fought
Like the war we just saw,
Within six months, our enemy would have been beat.
We wouldn't have suffered defeat.
When it looks easy, then it's planned right.
If it were so easy, why didn't you moaners
Say this before the war started.
This you didn't do, you joined the rest
And became a Monday morning quarterback.
Historians say this war is insignificant.
I said it before and I'll say it again,
Their opinions sound like someone drinking gin.
When one American life is lost, that isn't insignificant?
Ask the families of those who aren't coming back.
During World War II many bombs were dropped by us.
In this short war more were dropped.
How insignificant this seems to be.
Chemical warfare was a big threat.
Special uniforms were worn by us.
This was never done before.
Would they stand up or would a trooper die
With pain and agony showing in his eyes.
It was no Normandy or Kasserine.
Thank God for that,
If so many lives would have been lost.
The battle involved decoys, deceptions, hit and run,
Pumping false information into C.N.N.
And other ploys that made it appear
Another Normandy was here.
Our great leaders fooled them all.
C.N.N. too took the bait.
A mass invasion they thought was on.
It was a work of art done in a military way.
What more can I say.
If this is insignificant,

Then all you so-called historians
Should go back to school.
I recommend West Point. I associate with them.
You may learn something
And see how wrong you really are.
They are the best by far.
They moan and groan because
Twelve million dollars was spent
On a parade to welcome our troopers home.
They should thank the Good Lord we're able to do this.
If the troopers don't make it home,
The moaners and the groaners would be in a parade
With their hands tied behind their backs.
Enslaved they would be.
Then they'll say honor was due them.
Money doesn't matter as long as we
Can walk the streets free as can be.
Jesus Christ and King Solomon
Made this statement many years ago.
"You cannot worship both money and God,
Because if you do,
you're going to love one and hate the other."
What our gallant troopers did was Godly.
They freed a nation from bondage.
You moaners and groaners seem to have the other choice.
I would like to tell you what you can do with it
But I'll leave that up to your imagination.
To all of you who yell and scream
And knock our flag and military,
If our enemy ever beats us to the punch,
Think twice before you yell and scream,
It could be your last from that fatal blast.

WILLIE (THE WISP) PEP

He fought as a featherweight a few years back,
From Hartford, Connecticut he came.
He held the reins from forty-two to fifty-one.
His feats shall never be beat.
Pound for pound he was the best of the rest.
Two hundred twenty-nine victories were his,
Losing only eleven.
As long as boxing remains,
This record will always be his to claim.
He won his first sixty-two in a row.
After losing one,
Seventy-three were his back to back.
He went down several times,
But never for the count.
Lightning fast and quick on his feet,
He danced around with the grace of a gazelle,
Jabbing his foes many times before they
Could raise their arms and do any harm.
As great as he was, there's one thing he did
That will always cling to me.
During a round he bobbed and weaved
With electrifying speed,
A glove on him was never laid.
Willie took that one, but never threw a punch.
Conceited he never was,
A boxer he never knocked.
What more can I say, he stands alone
And shall never be dethroned.

43

THE INDIANS' PLIGHT

They were here first of all,
They planted seed, fished the stream,
Hunted game, to fill their frames.

The open land was theirs to keep,
To raise their own till fully grown.
The stars and sky was their roof above,
They loved to rove and not be told to stay on hold.

They bothered none and wanted fun,
To be left alone so they could roam.
We came along and did all wrong.
We didn't care who they were,
We cheated, beat, and killed those out there.

Even their small had to fall,
That didn't make us look too tall.
We did what we did, but the day will come,
When the sun will fall and then we'll see,
The wrong we did will never be hid.

THE SOUTH WOULD HAVE WON

The Civil War started in 1861.
Sad and tragic as can be,
Father fought son, brother against brother.
Twenty-one steps led to this tragedy.
Who was right and who was wrong
Remains a mystery,
Depending on whose side you're on.
One thing I know for sure,
If on even terms it were fought,
The South would have easily won.
The North had more manpower, firepower,
Cavalry, mass production and many assets
In their favor.
The South had better leaders, cavalry, fighters
And were fighting on their own terrain.
At the beginning they were winning.
Numbers and mass production beat them,
Otherwise on the battle field
They would have won.
The outcome would have been
Victory for those who suffered defeat.
Be careful how you judge.
For what they had
They didn't do too bad.
They were the best of the two.
History says it was the other way.
This I will never buy,
As sure as there are stars in the sky.

THE GALLANT GALLOP OF CO'S C-E-F-I-L

What Really Happened At The Little Big Horn,
Did Custer Have A Plan ?

He came through the coulee with 200 strong.
Not knowing whether he was right or wrong.
He knew they were there but he didn't care
For fear of death was never his fare.
On and on he trotted, he knew he had been spotted.
Glory, Honor, Victory were his all
If he could win here he would stand tall.
But fate has its way not Custer's to say.
Down he rode when shot as he strode.
He was the first to fall
And then there were more.
Their leader was gone.
Those that were left fled in despair.
For death filled the air, and all would fall
Never to hear that bugle call.

HE AND SHE

As God sits above we look in awe at that which he loves.
He cares for us all, that we may not fall,
But we are not He, and never will be.

We try to stand tall,
Next to Him we are small.
We try to do good and honor all,
But we are not He and so you see,
We are weak, and cause others to weep.

I tried to stand tall,
But had a great fall.
My love was strong,
I thought of no wrong,
But I am not He, as you can see.

I tried to do right,
But in my plight,
I was up tight.
I made her weep,
Because I was not He.
She is like He, a saint to me.
She'll never fall,
She will always stand tall.

For all that is said,
I hope above all,
That she will say, being like He,
Take my hand and come to me,
And you too can be like He.

YOUNG GIRL

It's been very hard on me
Loving you so much
Knowing it could never be.
I had to face reality.
You had youth and could
Do what you do.
I had to pine and bite my time.
Hope on hope would lead to despair.
You didn't care, for in your
Eyes I was never there.
I came too soon ahead of you
But what was I to do.
You were young and pretty as can be
Lovely as a blooming tree.
I had youth years ago
It won't last as you will see.
I never loved then as I do now,
My youth is gone but love remained.
So you see, how bad can it be.
In your need I was there to give you aid
After that you had your laugh.
So I must go on my way
And thank the Lord for that fine day
When love over youth had its say.

LONA LONA

Be my queen,
I love you more than life supreme.
As I get on bended knee,
Fill me with glee and say I love thee.
Tell me now, as I know not when,
He will say from above, you've done your all,
The war is on and you may fall,
Never to hear her loving call.

MARIA - ON THAT FINE DAY

Maria, Maria, I know what it is to be filled with bliss.
Your beauty alone is deeper than a kiss.
It comes to one that can never repay,
The joy you gave on that fine day.
The sun was shining, the air was clear.
It had to be, for you were there.
The clouds were gone and no rain had fallen.
It seems to me there was a certain calling.
Your outward beauty had its say,
As it kept the clouds away.
Your inward beauty came to play,
It can't be seen, from the heart it came,
On that fine day.
The sun glistened brightly above.
You made it stay and kept the rain away.
As you see it had to be,
You were with me and filled me with glee.
Your beauty from within can never be bought,
You're one of a kind and very hard to find.
I hope we'll repeat the day,
That shall never go away.
Thank you Maria for that fine day.

KIMBERLY

Do not despair for he's up there.
He will take your every care,
And make it pass like a blade of grass.
He knows what you went through,
To be ill is no thrill,
It would give anyone a chill.
As it goes, he knows your wants are his,
And will surely give you bliss.
So when you're well you can tell,
He was there to care for you.
The sun will shine and in due time,
I will take you out to dine.
Take care pretty little girl,
Hope to see you soon.

LISA

She turned twenty-seven
On February the seventeenth.
I wish her a happy twenty-seven
And many more to come.
She's as pretty as can be,
A beauty to behold.
Her eyes sparkle like stars in the sky.
When she walks about with such grace,
It seems like a cloud above
Is carrying her through space.
She's warm and carefree as can be.
She's a lot of fun and always on the run.
When I'm with her I'm as happy as can be.
She fills me with glee.
My heart jumps with joy.
She alone does this to me.
When we wine and dine
The pleasure is all mine.
I thank the good Lord
For being so kind.
It was by accident we met,
Maybe it was meant to be.
She inspires me in what I do.
The love she emits fills me with bliss.
I say to her thank you.
It's my honor knowing you.

CHRISTINE CHRISTINE

We have never met,
Yet when I call you
Your voice is one that
I shall never forget.
As it passes through the wire,
It sets my heart on fire.
I tingle with joy
Like a small boy playing with a toy.
You make my day
As you say words
That fill me with glee.
How I wish I could get
On bended knee and say I love thee.
Maybe it will come to pass
And we shall meet at last.
I don't know when
It will come about.
I am far away, but whatever
You say I'll wait for that day.
For if you love it doesn't care,
Even though it came over the air.

AMO TE VERA – My belle from Ontario

RHONDA

Tall and pretty as can be,
It's a treat to watch her
As she emcees on T.V.
She kids around and makes you laugh.
What she does is a real blast.
She struts about with the
Grace of a gazelle.
Her shinning eyes seem to put you in a spell.
She's very charming and gracious
As she models clothes on T.V.
The ones I like best are those she wears
When she honors our red, white, and blue.
On her they stand out alone.
She seems to have that special knack
That says don't look at me,
Look at the colors of our land of the free.
I guess it had to be, for you see,
She's on the U.S.A. station
Whose letters stand for our great nation.
It's my pleasure watching her
As she honors our stars and stripes
Brightening my day in every way.

HAPPY EASTER LISA

Beautiful as can be,
Your beauty also lies within
Because it came from Him.
You shine too, he told me so.
Maybe this you didn't know.
He in his own mysterious ways
Gave me something I never had,
It's Godly as can be.
A strong force that comes from above,
It's deep inside and fills me with pride.
I got a certain call, I don't know why
Only he can answer that.
What I did came from Him.
I honored many, it was their just due
As they fought for the Red, White and Blue.
He looked and smiled and said to me
Don't forget Lisa, she always stood by me.
Goodness and virtue she always had
When times were good and times were bad.
She held her own and let it be known
No matter what the case may be
She would always honor me.
In my palm she will stay
There is no other way.

MASTER DePALMA AND JOYCE

He's a kind, gentle man
From Wethersfield, Connecticut where I am.
He's as pleasant as can be,
But don't mess with him,
He holds the black belt fifth degree.
He'll tear you apart if you start
Trouble with him.
Down you'll go,
You'd think you were hit with
A ton of bricks.
He's my Karate instructor,
One of the best there is.
He's an ex-Marine and discipline
He well knows from the Corps
In what he does.
This he teaches us, also various holds,
How to hit and protect ourselves from our foes.
He's admired by all.
He also states
Karate is not only an offensive and defensive weapon,
It teaches us self-control, and helping others,
Things we do when passing through life.
He and Joyce are engaged to wed.
This fills me with bliss.
As sure as God made a tree,
This was meant to be.
But Joyce remember one thing,
He belongs to us all.
When you are one
Don't take him all the time,
Because good men like him are hard to find.

CASA LOMA RESTAURANT
HARTFORD, CONNECTICUT

Dedicated to:
The employees and customers who signed two large Christ-
mas and New Year card tablets, that were sent to the United
States First Cavalry in the Persian Gulf.

If you wish to wine and dine,
The food at the Casa Loma is mighty fine.
Paul and Tony, your congenial hosts,
Will greet you and seat you.
Italian dishes are their specialties.
There are other varieties.
Fish, steak, veal, and roast beef,
The Saturday night special.
No other eatery can compete
With this delicious piece of beef.
The service is fine,
Fast as can be.
There's also a banquet room
For parties, weddings, or
Whatever you may need.
A buffet you may have.
Whatever you prefer,
They will be happy to serve.
Your needs will be their every care.
When you leave you will be pleased
You came and had a good time,
Partaking of the fine food and wine.
When you come back,
Paul and Tony will cordially greet you
Saying - Enjoy yourself as you did
When you last dined.
The pleasure is ours,
If pleased you are.

GEORGE AND LISA

They were young and full of heart.
George and Lisa were their names.
When you saw them together you'd think
They were one as they got along so well
And always seemed to be having fun.
She loved him dearly, but his love for her
Was stronger than she ever knew.
He worshipped and adored her.
She was his star on high.
It mattered not who loved the most,
For they would have each other
Till the day they are called away.
George had to go off to war.
They said their good-byes.
He told her not to cry.
Into battle he went.
His thoughts were always of her.
He knew some day a small child would
Be theirs to have and hold,
But fate had its way,
Not George's to say.
A bullet struck him
And down he fell.
He looked up to the sky before he died,
And said good Lord above
Take care of my Lisa
Till we meet again
In that place where all is good
And there is no sin.

PROSE

OUR BOYS AND GIRLS ARE DYING FOR OUR FLAG

U.S. Supreme Court Why?

Well, well, the Supreme Court does it again. First the atheists and agnostics who say there is no God, want open prayers in public schools thrown out and the Supreme Court rules in their favor. Now the Supreme Court says it's all right to burn the American flag and get away with it.

Next they will be telling us to take the word God off our monies, or no more prayers on the opening and closing sessions of the United States Congress. Or, you don't have to stand up while our National Anthem is being played. The best one I would say is that you can't say "God Bless You" when someone sneezes.

To lay the cards on the table, I respect the Supreme Court of the United States, but the way it is going presently, I don't have to respect the people in it.

As the Constitution is being interpreted today, it is nothing but a legal handbook of loopholes for criminals to commit murder, rape, push dope, etc. and get away with it. The Constitution is not being used, it is being abused.

Supreme Court, I believe you made a serious blunder when you took open prayers out of public schools. You went along with a bunch of hypocrites. They say there is no God, and their Constitutional rights are being violated. That seems very strange, for the simple reason when you're in combat and under enemy attack, and those mortar and artillery shells are coming in on you, you will never see an atheist in a *foxhole*. All you will hear is "*God* save me" and the *Our Father*, and let me see if you can guess who is saying this.

The way the Supreme Court has been ruling these past years is a disgrace to the brave and gallant men and women who gave their lives for their *God* and their *flag*.

Supreme Court, if you wish to verify what I'm saying, take a walk through the Veteran's Hospitals throughout the country and talk to the combat veterans who lost arms or legs and have other serious combat wounds. Ask them what they think about their *God* and their *flag*.

I was in the Army during the Korean War, or conflict, whichever you prefer. I'm 58 years old. If I have to, I will fight and die if I'm called again to defend *God's honor, my flag,* and *my country.*

Supreme Court, where's our Yankee Doodle Dandy?

Have you read Barbara Frietchie? *"Shoot if you must this old gray head, but spare your country's flag."* General Robert E. Lee, our enemy, looked at her and turned to his soldiers and said whoever touches a hair of yon gray head dies like a dog. March on men. This 90-year-old brave lady put her life on the line to preserve her country's flag. What's more mind-boggling is the fact that Robert E. Lee was going to kill his own men if any harm came to that brave lady or our flag. Supreme Court, could you do what either of these did to honor the flag which is us, our free country. I doubt it very much. Think about that.

I have never seen the Constitution carried into combat, only our beautiful Old Glory. Our flag was born in 1777, our country. The Constitution was created in 1789. The flag came first. Without the flag, there is no Constitution. The flag made the Constitution possible. Our fallen boys and girls are the stars in the Red, White, and Blue. Give them their due honor.

Kate Smith said it better than anyone. *"God Bless America, land that I love."*

> Sincerely,
> George Shea
> Your Connecticut Yankee Doodle Dandy
> Wethersfield, Connecticut

THE EMANCIPATION PROCLAMATION

The Emancipation Proclamation didn't free the slaves.
When I was in school years back, I was taught that President
Lincoln's Emancipation Proclamation freed the slaves.
I imagine many of you were taught the same thing. This is
completely false. It didn't free the slaves as I shall
explain.

Under the Constitution, slavery was legal in the states where
it was established. The Emancipation Proclamation was issued
January first eighteen sixty-three. The South had seceded
from the Union in eighteen sixty-one. Therefore not being
part of the Union, the Proclamation had no jurisdiction over
the southern states. The slaves remained slaves. They were
never freed. One thing and one thing only freed the slaves.
That was the thirteenth amendment to the United States
Constitution in eighteen sixty-five. The fourteenth made
them citizens and the fifteenth gave them the right to vote.
The Constitution freed the slaves not the Emancipation
Proclamation.

CUSTER'S 7TH

*This following article and poem is written in rebuttal to
an article that states Custer's 7th lost its honors and
they can now be restored in the Persian Gulf War. Don't
believe this at all, as I shall explain. Honors were
never lost. It seems we have another pseudo expert type
Monday morning quarterback as we have just seen on CNN.
They speak with forked tongue.*

This is an open letter to the First Squadron 7th Regiment
U.S. 1st Cavalry. You squad leaders and officers I wish you would
read this letter to your troopers, as I have sent thousands of my
articles to our troopers in Arabia and various organizations in
this country. I won't have enough to go around. First of all,
our country wishes to thank you and all your troopers for a job
well done. We love you and honor you. Words can't describe what
we feel for you. When you come home you will see parades,
rallies, flags, and yellow ribbons that will boggle your mind.
You deserve all this praise and more. "God Bless You All".

Now troopers I would like to clear the air concerning things
said about General Custer. This article enclosed is completely
false as are many things said about Custer. The 7th never lost
its honor. I will tell you why. Custer, by doing what he did,
saved Terry's command of 400 from getting wiped out. He also had
an ingenious plan of attack. My book is nearly finished. A
factual movie is going to be made on it. What I write I prove or
don't write it. My findings have been verified by military
experts at West Point and 1st Cavalry Horse Detachment, Ft. Hood,
Texas, not by these so-called Monday morning quarterbacks and so
called experts that we had then and still have now. As you see
what was falsely stated about Custer by these so-called experts
was stated in the battle you were in. I describe it more so in
the epic poem I wrote about your gallant 7th.

When my book is read by the public and the movie is made,
General Custer's 7th and your 7th will be the most honored
regiment in the U.S. Army. That I *Promise you*. Very few military
experts and Custer authorities have seen my plans for
precautionary reasons. Can't let the cat out of the bag. They
claim that when my book is out, they will have to rewrite the
books on Custer. History will be changed. So troopers, hold your
heads high and fill yourself with pride - The 7th will never die.

Now I'm going to tell you what I'm all about concerning my book on Custer. I can't tell you everything, as I have to have something for my book. At the Court of Inquiry in 1879 Reno and Benteen (by the way, this was a kangaroo court) state that Custer believed there was no hostile camp ahead. This is very interesting indeed. When Custer reaches the Lone Tepee, he sends thirty-five Ree Scouts to capture the hostiles' ponies. If Custer believes there is no camp, then why does he send the Ree Scouts to capture the ponies. Where are the ponies coming from? What do we have here, ghost riders in the sky. It has never been challenged in 115 years by anyone. They don't know why, but I do.

At 12:15 p.m., Custer sends Benteen left oblique. Why this formation? It has never been explained by anyone. I know why. He sends Benteen, a Captain, on the mission before Reno, a Major. According to the chain of command, Reno should have gone, but he didn't, never explained. I know why. Custer has over forty Indian scouts. He takes several and the rest go with Reno. Benteen is going into no man's land and yet Custer doesn't give him one scout. Why? I know why. Custer splits his regiment into three fighting battalions. He has three doctors with him. I asked people, over 300 in all walks of life, military and civilian, how they would disperse the doctors. They all said one to each battalion, but what does Custer do. He keeps one and Reno has two. He was the decoy. He would have more wounded than others. Custer doesn't give one doctor to Benteen. Are the bullets and arrows supposed to bounce off his troopers. Custer knew there were no hostiles in Benteen's path and there weren't. He knew in due time Benteen would pull into the main trail and this is what he does. Custer knew everything that he was doing. What I have just stated is all a part of Custer's plan. Read Custer's message to Benteen, that tells you a lot. It took me months to break it down logistically and now I know what it means exactly.

Maybe I shouldn't be saying this, but I take pride in myself. The glory belongs to you troopers. In doing my book the past years I verified many things at West Point D.M.I. and 1st Cavalry Horse Detachment, Ft. Hood, Texas. Growing up I excelled in History and battles. Everything else I stunk at. Several weeks back I told West Point that I had a plan that could be used against Hussein. They told me to call the Pentagon Deputy Chief of Staff, which I did. I told them my situation. They told me to send maps and plans to them, which I did. The plans involved decoys, deceptions and night fighting. If you will see how the attack took place, all these tactics were used, so I'm rather proud that I was in the ball park area. I'm greatly honored that the Pentagon would accept and look at my plans. These people are the greatest military minds in the world. I thank them, for deep in my heart, I didn't want to lose one of our gallant troopers to that mad man. So you see troopers, what I write about Custer I verify. Here are some of my experts - Major Stephen Foster, Captain Barron, D.M.I., Department of Military Instruction, West Point. Colonel Tom Larkin Retired, Army Horse Detachment, Instructor, 1st Cavalry, Ft. Hood, Texas. Captain John Roper - now serving in Arabia with the U.S. 1st Cavalry. Steve Alexander, the Civilian who portrays Custer, knows more about the man than anyone, Custer consultant.

Well, troopers that's it for now. God Bless You. We all love you and are proud of you.

George Shea
March 4, 1991
Wethersfield, Connecticut

THE U.S. 7TH RIDES ON

On a Sunday years ago
The U.S. 7th Cavalry
Under the command of Colonel Custer
Engaged the Sioux and Cheyenne in Montana,
The Battle of the Little Big Horn.
He was bold, daring, and cocky as can be.
Many have said that caused his defeat.
Don't believe this at all.
This didn't cause him to fall.
He had to attack and gave himself up
Saving General Terry's 400 from biting the dust.
This I have proven and will challenge
Anyone that can say, it didn't happen that way.
Years ago there were writers, historians and
So-called experts that put Custer down.
You have the same people today.
You saw this on T.V.
President Bush was called a wimp.
He was also the head of the C.I.A.
50,000 troopers or more were to die
If they attacked on the ground.
The Marines were to attack from the sea.
How wrong can these people be.
So you see what was said falsely about Custer,
The same was said about the battle across the sea.
As it was true then, it is true now.
These so-called experts should throw in the towel.
The 7th is over there
Fighting for you and me
So that we will always be free.
They will hold their own and let it be known
They will bring honor and glory
To the same colors long ago.
When General Custer fought and died
To save those who would have never survived that Sunday.
The choice was his.
There was no other way.
Terry's command was saved to fight another day.
Troopers when your colors go passing by,
Hold your heads up high.

THE PENTAGON

What is the Pentagon and what's involved? We know it's in Washington, D.C. It employs about 30,000 people or more. The building is very large and militarily oriented, but somewhere along the way we don't seem to understand what this building means. We miss the bottom line. I would say we take this building for granted and this is a great falsity on our part and this falsity we don't need.

It is not only a building in itself and people. It is a certain kind of building and has certain people in it. Here you have the smartest and ablest military minds in the world, from all branches of the service. During peace time, they plan and layout our defenses. If we are on the brink of war, they plan our offense, and during wartime, they plan the whole ball game. These leaders are the best and most capable that this country has to offer. These people are highly underrated when it comes to war as we see it today. They are behind the scenes and usually don't get the credit due to them. During World War II, you heard of our great generals winning the battles and getting all the glory which they rightly deserved, but those that made it possible were George C. Marshall and his staff at the Pentagon. They planned the battles, and in some cases a field general had to make a decision on his own, but again the plans were laid out by the Pentagon. In this war we just had, General Powell, as in Marshall's case, had to plan the attack. Under General Powell there were junior officers and others who had to put together their expertise to make the plan of attack possible. These people we never hear of, but without them we don't go. Everything was put together by all, and because of this we came out victorious. There's an expression used in horse racing, and it goes something like this. The horse makes the trainer, the trainer doesn't make the horse. The same thing may be said here. Those that work in the Pentagon (the horses) make those generals (trainers) in the field of combat look real good, because of this, victory is ours. But the trainers always get the praise and glory and not the horses.

But as you can see
As the case may be.
You see but you do not perceive
There can only one answer be.
It's there in D.C.
In a place called the Pentagon.
They were able to foresee and
Plan a great victory for you and me.
Because of them and what they do
A good night's sleep we shall have.
We thank the good Lord
For they saw the light and
Did everything right.

OUR BEAUTIFUL OLD GLORY

The flag burners think they have won. The Supreme Court of the United States seems to agree with them. Even members of the Congress of the United States go along with them also. They too went against the flag burning amendment. Senator Dole was correct when he stated that there are too many lawyers in Congress and not enough Americans.

Let's see if we can put the priorities where they belong and see who is right and who is wrong. On July Fourth 1776 we broke away from England. From 1776 to 1781 American blood was spilled and on June l4th 1777 the American flag was born because of the American blood that was spilled. The country and the flag held on. Because of this in 1789 the Articles of the Confederation were created - "The Constitution of the United States."

The point is if the American flag doesn't make it and the spilled blood was in vain, there is no Constitution. The flag and the spilled blood made the Constitution possible. The Constitution never made the flag — without the flag there is no Constitution. I have never seen the Constitution being waved or carried into combat when the enemy is being attacked. All I see is our beautiful "Old Glory" standing tall as can be and saying I'm here as I was there way back when, because you cared for me.

LETTERS

March 20, 1991

Dear Mr. Shea:

Thank you for your message about the United States efforts in the Persian Gulf region. This was not a war we wanted, but there are times in the life of our country when we confront principles worth fighting for; this was one such time.

The cooperation of the community of nations in stopping Saddam Hussein's ruthless aggression and in liberating Kuwait is unprecedented. Certainly I am pleased that the ground war ended in one hundred hours and that there were far fewer casualties than had been widely predicted. Operation Desert Storm's success belongs to our courageous troops. We are all tremendously proud of them, and I am delighted that they are coming home to the hero's welcome that they deserve.

As we assume our responsibility as a catalyst for peace and stability in the Middle East region, we will not forget those who gave their lives for this just cause, those who lost loved ones, or those innocent people who have suffered as a result of this conflict. I ask for your prayers for all those thus affected and for continued blessings on our great Nation.

Sincerely,

George Bush

Mr. George Shea
15 Morrison Avenue
Wethersfield, Connecticut 06109

6 April 1991

Dear Mr. Shea,

I want to express my sincere thanks for your letter and poems voicing support for our valiant troops. The tremendous outpouring of encouragement by the American people has been the foundation and driving force behind our success in both Operation Desert Shield and Operation Desert Storm.

You and thousands like you have provided us the strength and determination to liberate Kuwait and fulfill the United Nations Resolutions. It is because of this visible demonstration of concern for our soldiers, sailors, airmen, marines and coastguardsmen that we in the military are proud to be serving our country and its citizens.

Again, thank you as we look forward to the day when our last servicemember returns to the shores of our great nation.

Sincerely,

H. NORMAN SCHWARZKOPF
General, U.S. Army

Mr. George Shea
15 Morrison Avenue
Wethersfield, CT 06109

DEPARTMENT OF THE ARMY
HEADQUARTERS, XVIII AIRBORNE CORPS AND FORT BRAGG
FORT BRAGG, NORTH CAROLINA 28307-5000

REPLY TO
ATTENTION OF: Colonel George Shea
15 Morrison Ave
Wethersfield, CT. 06109

Dear George,

How are you? This is your buddy, Spec. Hargrave.
But please, call me Jim. Thank you for your continued
letters and poems-they certainly mean a alot to me
and my countrymen.

Your poems and letters of patriotism have certainly
helped soldiers, seamen, and airman all over the
world through this whole ordeal. Although I wish that
it didn't have to take a war for people to have faith
in their country. People should fly the flag even in
times of peace. There's nothing like getting up in
the morning and seeing "Old Glory" flying to beat the
band.

I wish you continued success on your book and movie,
and hope you will continue to write me. I do enjoy
receiving your packages and phone calls. Please accept
this letter and included package with my best regards.
Take care-

Your friend,

James H. Hargrave ESQ.

Specialist James Hargrave
XVIII Abn Corps and Fort Bragg
Public Affairs Office

70

DEPARTMENT OF THE ARMY

HEADQUARTERS, 24TH INFANTRY DIVISION (MECHANIZED) AND FORT STEWART
FORT STEWART, GEORGIA 31314-5000

REPLY TO
ATTENTION OF

Public Affairs Office   February 14, 1991

Mr. George Shea
15 Morrison Avenue
Wethersfield, CT 06109

Dear Mr. Shea:

    I would like to thank you for both your concern for our
soldiers in Saudi Arabia and the poems written on their
behalf. The support of individuals such as yourself is what
keeps our soldiers dedicated and their determination strong.
I will forward them to my counterpart in the 24th Infantry
Division (Mechanized).

    Again, thank you and best wishes for the success of your
upcoming book and movie. Your patriotism is appreciated.

                        Sincerely,

                        DONALD W. KEELING
                        Major, Field Artillery
                        Public Affairs Officer

DISABLED AMERICAN VETERANS

NATIONAL HEADQUARTERS • P.O. BOX 14301 • CINCINNATI, OHIO 45250-0301 • (606) 441-7300

April 2, 1991

Colonel George Shea
15 Morrison Avenue
Wethersfield, CT 06109

Dear Colonel Shea:

Thank you so much for sharing your poetry with us here at the National Head-
quarters of the Disabled American Veterans. We are very appreciative of all who
support our organization.

I will use these in two ways:

1. A copy of your works is being forwarded to our editorial offices at DAV
   Magazine. I'm sure they will read them with interest - especially the
   fact that General Powell has had one of your poems laminated for his
   wall.

2. I will retain a copy for possible use in our fundraising copy - the
   letters and inserts to our appeals for donations to the Disabled
   American Veterans. It is possible that your poetry can provide valuable
   input as our organization seeks to provide the highest degree of service
   to America's disabled veterans and their families.

Once again, we're very appreciative of the time you took to share your ideas
with us. Please be assured that we will try to use your poetry as we seek ways
to fully meet the needs of the veterans and families we serve.

Sincerely,

Bruce D. McLeaster
Assistant Manager of Direct Mail

CC: J. Atchison - DC

Captain J.W. Roper
8th Combat Engineers
1st Cavalry
Desert Storm, Kuwait

Dear George —

Thank you so much for your kind letter and copies of your prose. I handed them out to squad leaders within the unit, and the troops were impressed and more than a few chests pumped up as they realized the significance of our historical ties to our cavalry forbears. Thanks again.

Respectfully,

John Roper

242 Trumbull Street
Hartford, Connecticut 06103
(203) 728-3366

January 31, 1991

George Shea
15 Morrison Avenue
Wethersfield, CT 06109

Dear George:

Thanks for the letter and the poems. They are an inspiration.

Maybe at some point this season I can use one of them in GOAL Magazine. If I do, I will send you a copy.

The letter on the flag burners is terrific. It hits things right on the nose.

Once again, thanks for writing.

Kind regards,

Phil Langan
Director of Public Relations

mlg/2757M

For Season Tickets, Ticket Plans and Group Sales Call 1-800-WHALERS

NEWSPAPERS

Towns People

President Responds to Patriot Shea's Poetry

By Joyce Rossignol
Editor

George Shea has heard from George Bush.

George Shea, who lives on Morrison Avenue, wrote a poem praising the president for the way he conducted the Gulf War.

This past week, President Bush wrote back, thanking Mr. Shea for his message.

George Shea has also written a poem entitled: "Thank You General Stormin' Norman" whom he describes as "the general who did it right" and a poem praising Chief of Staff General Colin Powell as "a shining star in or midst."

He's written poems about Marine Lance Corporal Daniel Byron Walker and Specialist Cindy M. Beaudoin, who gave their lives in the Persian Gulf War.

Though he's always loved poetry, he never wrote any until now. "I can't believe it; it's just a call, I guess," he said as he is moved to create more patriotic verses to praise and comfort the troops who served in the Persian Gulf,

their leaders and their families.

A disabled veteran of the Korean Conflict himself, Mr. Shea has always been obsessed with history and America. Even as a student at Bulkeley High School he was, he says, a genius in history and not bad at baseball either. "But I was dumb in everything else," he says. He can still recite dates and facts and battle plans.

He shared his knowledge of military strategy with the Pentagon just two weeks before the final battle in the Gulf that was constructed almost exactly as he suggested in his letters of Jan. 30 and Feb. 14.

Before he was so moved by the war in the Gulf, he had been researching General Custer's Battle of Little Bighorn. He wrote to the Pentagon that "we can catch the enemy off guard and nail him when he least expects it. We shall do what the Sioux and Cheyenne did many years ago. They were masters of the decoy, deception, hit and run."

"Hussein wants a ground attack. We shall

give him one, but there's a catch. We are not going to use any ground troops.

"By hitting them on the front lines in one grand attack, they will believe we are to launch a ground attack, and this is what we want. Our tanks can see the enemy at night but the enemy can't see them. They can hit a target miles away with pinpoint accuracy."

He proposed that the allied forces pretend to be planning an attack by sea. "Let the barges go in close to shore."

He proposed fooling the Iraqis with tapes of bugles and yelling, heavy artillery, tanks being blown up, simulating and attack. He suggested using CNN to report what the enemy saw during this simulation.

"The Indians were very clever, after all," Mr. Shea wrote to the Pentagon.

He should know. He's been studying Custer's Last Stand for the past three years and George Shea says, General Custer did have a plan, that history has not been fair to Custer."

Mr. Shea hopes to right

that wrong. He is working on a book that he hopes may be made into a documentary film, telling the truth about General Custer's final battle, that Custer's last stand saved General Terry's command of 400 men. "Custer didn't go in there recklessly," Mr. Shea says. "He had no choice."

He is not alone in this: Custer experts stretch across the country and include film producer Lawson Warren, in Nashville, Tennessee, and Steve Alexander, the actor who portrays General Custer at the tourist attraction at Little Big Horn. Both will be involved in the documentary that may be made from George Shea's book.

He has written poems and letters to the present 1st Cavalry, 7th Regiment, that is said to be haunted still by what happened at Little Big Horn. Defending General Custer, Mr. Shea urged the 7th Regiment cavalry scouts who were guiding the Allied Troops into Kuwait to: "hold your heads up high/ when your colors go passing by."

Mr. Shea has always been a patriot. When he was in the military he was in the Presidential Honor Guard at the Tomb of the Unknown Soldier at Arlington, VA. "We were the sharpest company in the U.S. Army," he says proudly.

Disabled in the Korean Conflict, George Shea has kept a relatively low profile until now. He is involved with his family's antique business in Wethersfield. He's pursued a particular interest in antique firearms.

The last three years he's spent a lot of time researching the Battle of Little Big Horn, Custer's Last Stand.

He praises the Wethersfield Library for its help. He's had help from Wethersfield High School, too. He's travelled to West Point, to the Carlisle War College, to Ft. Hood, Texas, and to Little Big Horn, where he scouted the terrain.

He's been made an associate member of the 1st Cavalry. "That's quite an honor," he said.

"Half of the stuff in the movies about Custer is bull crap," he said. "Custer didn't charge in not knowing what he was doing."

He said he should have been a history teacher, but after graduating from Bulkeley High School in 1951, and two years at the University of Connecticut, he went into the Army, and came back disabled.

His Custer research is on hold right now not so much by choice but because he can't stop writing poems and letters to the heroes of the Persian Gulf.

He does expect to get back to his book on Custer soon and to see it through to a documentary film. "The battle of Little Big Horn is the most talked about, written about and misunderstood battle in the history of the United States," he says. He hopes to correct the misunderstanding.

ACKNOWLEDGMENTS

I would like to thank the following people and businesses for the help given to me during our trying times putting my first book together.

Paul Gipstein-Hill Crest Promotions, Wethersfield, CT
Debra Drena-Proof Reader, Wethersfield, CT
Susan Parsons-Proof Reader, Wethersfield, CT
Gloria Kiel-English Teacher, Bloomfield, CT
Colonel John Chester Fife and Drum Corps, Wethersfield, CT
Brian Groves-Photogragher, Newington, CT
Jan Zablocki-Typist, Wethersfield, CT
Steve Tiberio-Wethersfield Offset Copy Center, Hartford, CT
Joe Amaio-Wethersfield Offset, Rocky Hill, CT
Ed Daly-Daly Forms & Type, Rocky Hill, CT
Wethersfield Public Library, Wethersfield, CT
Cora J. Belden Library, Rocky Hill, CT
Hartford Public Library, Hartford, CT
John Kulick Show-Channel 32, Rocky Hill, CT
Readers' Book Store, Rocky Hill, CT
Books Unlimited, Rocky Hill, CT
Wethersfield High School Faculty, Wethersfield, CT
Steve Alexander-General Custer Consultant, Jackson, Michigan
Homer Babbidge Library-The University of Connecticut, Storrs, CT
Ohio State University Library, Columbus, Ohio
Service Group Inc.-Wethersfield CT